THE GREAT WHITE SHARK

ANIMAL BOOKS FOR KIDS AGE 9-12

Children's Animal Books

The great white shark looks and acts scary! Is it dangerous to us when we go swimming? Read on and learn more about this amazing fish.

Smiling great white shark.

MEET THE GREAT WHITE SHARK

Great white sharks are the largest predatory fish in the ocean. They eat animals and other fish, rather than eating plankton and other small sea creatures and plants. They grow about fifteen feet long, although some much bigger great white sharks have been seen.

These sharks live and hunt off the coasts of every continent except Antarctica. However, the largest number patrol the seas near South Africa. The sharks prefer cooler, shallower water, and so there are fewer of them away from the coastlines or in the tropics.

Great White Shark.

Great white sharks, and five other shark species, are endothermic. That means they can raise their body temperature above the temperature of the water they are in. This lets them swim deeper and in colder waters than other sharks can tolerate.

These shark giants generally live and hunt on their own, although they gather in mating season and sometimes to hunt together. They can live as long as seventy-five years.

Predator of the sea.

HOW THEY LIVE

Great white shark mothers usually have a litter of ten or a dozen babies, after being pregnant for almost a year. Scientists think that a female great white has a litter every two years, but nobody knows for sure.

As soon as the sharks are born, they swim away from their mother and the other sharks. Great whites have no affection of their babies, and will eat them just like any other prey. Even before they are born, the larger baby sharks in the womb may attack and eat the smaller, weaker ones. This is called *"Oophagy"*.

The baby sharks are about five feet long at birth, and are able to hunt and defend themselves as soon as they are in the water. The babies, or pups, eat fish, squid, and other small sea creatures as they grow. When they reach adulthood, they prefer attacking and eating sea mammals, like seals, sea lions and even small whales. They will also attack and eat other great whites, even other adults when they are fighting over territory.

Male great whites are adults by about ten years of age; females become mature after about fifteen years, and usually grow to be much larger than the males.

Great White Shark breaching in an attack.

HOW THEY HUNT

Great whites have extremely good senses, so they can detect prey over a great distance under water. They can smell a colony of seals from as much as two miles away, and they can sense blood in the ocean from as much as three miles away.

In fact, great whites have six senses, one more than the five we humans get by on. They use sight, smell, touch, taste, hearing and electroreception. This last sense lets them feel electromagnetic vibrations in the water caused by the activity of other creatures. When they are close to their prey, great whites can sense the animal's heartbeat even if it is staying very still.

The Great White Shark's attack.

Great whites like to hunt early in the morning, when visibility is poor. This means other sea creatures have less of a chance of seeing the approaching shark.

SPY-HOPPING AND BREACHING

As the shark draws close to prey that is on or near the surface, it may *"spy-hop"*, popping its head above the water to get a clear look at what it is closing in on.

When they actually attack, great whites can "breach" like a whale, jumping as much as ten feet out of the water. This means that even sea birds are not safe from great whites! Sometimes when they do this, the sharks come down by accident on the deck of a boat! Since a great white shark weighs about a ton, that can be bad for the boat.

SURPRISE!

It is hard for fish and sea mammals to see a great white, as their bodies are *"counter-shaded"*. This means they are darker on the top and lighter on the bottom. When you are above a great white, looking down, the shark's body blends into the darker water below it. When you are below the shark, looking up, its lighter belly blends with the light filtering down from the sky.

Often, great whites move in slowly to a position below the seal or other creature they want to attack. Then the shark swims upward quickly, grabbing the prey in its mouth and breaching to stun and confuse the victim. They crash back into the water, shaking the victim the way a dog shakes a small animal it has caught.

NO CHEWING

Sharks don't chew their food. They bite off chunks and swallow them as a lump. Often they will attack an animal, taking a bite and leaving a serious wound, and then swim away for a bit, returning once the prey is weakened to finish it off.

A BIG APPETITE

A great white can eat as much as eleven tons of food in a year. When great whites can't find prey to attack, they will eat from the carcasses of dead animals. However, they can go for as much as three months between big meals.

Great White Shark in attack.

DO THEY HUNT PEOPLE?

There are records, and many wild stories, about great white sharks attacking humans. Although great whites do attack people, it is very rare.

In the 20th century, there are records of 108 great white shark attacks on people on the coasts of the United States, or just over one a year. Only eight of those people died. Scientists say that the attacks are almost always *"curiosity biting"*, and that once the great white finds out what it has bitten, it generally gives up and goes hunting for other prey.

One of the reasons for that is that humans are too bony and take too long to digest. It is easier for the great white to find food that sits more easily in its stomach than to try to digest your leg or arm!

Scientists say there is a great difference between the way a great white approaches a seal or other prey it recognizes, and the way it approaches a person in the water. As described, the great white attacks a seal at great speed, often breaching high out of the water once it has the seal in its mouth. By contrast, people attacked by great whites report that the shark approached slowly, almost in a lazy fashion.

Underwater great white shark approaching a swimmer.

Sharks use their mouths as we use our hands, to find out about things. Most great white attacks on people are puncture wounds as the shark tests out this strange thing in the water. When the person turns out to be more trouble than it is worth as food, the great white usually lets him go and goes on its way in search of something better to eat.

Great whites do attack boats, and sometimes tip them over. This may be because their electrorecepton sense gets confused by the electric fields the boat's motor and electronic equipment generates.

SHARP SHARK FACTS

Here are some sharp facts about great white sharks to sink your teeth into!

- Great white shark fossils have been found from more than 16 million years ago, and they could be a much older species than that.

- Great whites, when attacking, can hit speeds up to 35 mph.

- The biting force of a great white's jaws is ten times the biting force of a lion.

- Great whites have five rows of teeth in their mouth, with 46 teeth in every row. As teeth get worn or broken, they are replaced by new teeth. Each tooth is knife-sharp, and has a serrated edge which helps the shark tear at the thing it has in its mouth.

- The largest great white tooth found so far was about as long as the width of a human hand.

Trio of Orcas (Killer Whales)

SHARKS IN DANGER

Sharks are great hunters and killers, but they also can be prey. They are a favorite food of killer whales, and sometimes of larger sharks.

When a killer whale attacks a great white, it rams the shark over and over to stun the shark and flip it on its back. In this position, the great white falls into a state called *"toxic immobility"* and cannot move or even breathe. Then the killer whale can easily eat it.

The other great threat to great whites is humans. People hunt the great whites on purpose, and often accidentally catch and kill them in nets set for fish.

People have tried to keep great white sharks in aquariums, but the sharks cannot survive in confinement. They stop eating, and may keep banging their heads into the aquarium walls until they die.

When a great white detects the blood of another great white shark in the water, it immediately heads away from that area. Sometimes it continues for hundreds of miles before it feels it has reached safety.

THE VAST, SALT SEA

Learn more about the oceans, and who lives in them, in Baby Professor books like *Ocean Tides and Tsunamis* and *Just Keep Swimming!*

Visit
BABY PROFESSOR
EDUCATION KIDS
www.BabyProfessorBooks.com
to download Free Baby Professor eBooks and view
our catalog of new and exciting Children's Books